REAL LEADERSHIP MATTERS

How We Choose Our Leaders
and Why

Rob Day

AP
ATRIUM
PRESS

Atrium Press
2120 S Reserve St #108
Missoula, Montana 59801
www.RealLeadershipMatters.com

Real Leadership Matters by Rob Day. -- 1st edition.
ISBN: 978-1-7347511-0-9 (hardcover)
ISBN: 978-1-7347511-1-6 (paperback)

Printed in United States of America

*"The government you elect
is the government you deserve."*

— THOMAS JEFFERSON

"All the great things are simple."

— WINSTON CHURCHILL

Contents

Author's Note

I've spent much of my life around leaders, whether they were in government, business, the military or the community. At the age of eighteen I was writing speeches in Washington for William Proxmire, historically one of our most prominent Senators. Ten years later, during the mid 1980's, I found myself spending the weekend at the Vermont home of Bill Odom, the then Director of the National Security Agency, discussing global affairs and career paths. He was a Lieutenant General, with an Ivy League PhD and a professor at several Ivy League universities. He once said to me, "Rob, my secret is that as a General, all the academics think I'm powerful, and as a Professor, all the military guys think I'm smart." One thing I learned early on about leaders, is they often, if not always, have multiple talents and interests and could have taken equally successful paths in many different directions.

Soon thereafter, I was working on Wall Street representing some of the greatest dealmakers of our time. Since then, as my business career evolved, I've worked with a great number of leaders, competed against them, advised them, learned from them, partnered with them and observed them; from presidents to prime ministers, CEOs and generals to royalty and ruling families.

Over time, I've come to realize that all leaders have certain attributes in common, some to a greater degree than others, and some more obvious than others, regardless of background, heritage, station, culture or country. Through this book, I aim to explore the attributes of leadership, and offer a lens and framework through which to view and evaluate our potential political leaders, analyze what it takes to be a leader, and offer some ideas about where great leaders, with the right vision, can take us.

Most of all, I seek to encourage thought and dialogue about how best to choose our leaders, since it is one of the few choices we can make that actually has the greatest impact on our daily lives. We cannot choose our parents, siblings or our children. But we can choose our leaders, so we should do it deliberately and thoughtfully, because getting it right, really does matter. Ultimately, through this book, I offer to share what I've learned, and help make it easier for us all to select the best leaders we can, and make certain we get the ones we deserve.

Rob Day
Missoula, Montana
March, 2020

Introduction

In this book, I aim to address three problems facing America today:

1) Identify and define what makes a good leader;
2) Define the elements of a clear vision that works for America; and
3) Show how we can pay for that vision.

In a world that is becoming increasingly fragmented and polarized, especially as we navigate through election cycles here in the U.S., and around the world, I thought it might be useful to offer a way of looking at things to help bring order to the chaos, and manage the confusion, so that we can choose our leaders wisely, and not randomly. Ultimately, so that we can choose the great leaders we deserve, and we can understand where we might be heading as a nation.

Because it is so easy to generate and receive information in this world of networked devices, the volume of information we face is large, travels fast and is dynamic. As a result, distortion becomes a major problem for society. For voters, separating the wheat from the chaff, the valuable from the useless, determining what is fake and what is real, is the challenge. For leaders, generating the signal, so people can find it in all the noise, becomes the challenge. Sending a clear message that connects with people is, however, essential.

As we go to the polls to choose our leaders, we are faced with many choices: good ones, and not so good ones. Reasonable people all agree we want to choose the good ones. So how do we do that? What process do we use to increase our chances of "getting it right"? There is a way to look at this challenge that makes it relatively easy to meet.

First, we need to identify our leaders, then focus on their message and finally make sure their message is realistic and achievable. If we don't have a good leader in the first instance, it doesn't much matter what the message is. And if the message is great, but unattainable, it's pretty much useless. In short, we need a great leader, with real solutions to our problems and a way to pay for those solutions.

Being from Montana, and a fly fisherman, I can't help but view today's candidates as anglers, trying to choose the right fly to attract and catch the elusive rainbow trout. The good anglers are able to match the pattern to the hatch, cast it elegantly into the pool where the noses rise, and successfully set the hook. Instead, I see questionable casting, and some very odd pattern choices, that don't really match the hatch and just bore or scare off the fish. Where are the great anglers, and how do we find them?

Now, please lean in, and listen carefully to a word of caution. If I could whisper in writing, I would. The American primary system is both confusing and dysfunctional. It's like a political genie let out of the bottle: once free, he is a smiling whirling dervish of mischievous activity that wreaks havoc in a subtly destructive way which seems almost innocent, except for its ultimate effect.

Primary voters are, for the most part, those who are paying attention, engaged and active. They comprise a relatively small percentage of the electorate – say 15% on average. They are also very often fervent ideologues, who represent the extremes of our two-party system. Not surprisingly, they tend to vote for those who are like-minded, or at least masquerade as like-minded, in order to attract the primary voters' support. This makes it very difficult for a truly moderate candidate to emerge successful from this process. Consequently, we can end up with relatively extreme candidates in the general elections. This is not a mystery. In the modern political era, it is well established that a successful candidate will run to the extremes in the primary, and then scramble like crazy to the middle, prevaricating, and artfully disavowing that other fellow who shared his name and somehow took over his mind and body during the primary. That necessarily means that together with the other 85% of the voting population, we run the risk of ending up with an extremist, a master prevaricator, a fraud or worse, as a titular leader. But we don't necessarily end up with what we thought we bargained for and deserve: a real leader.

Whether we choose to admit it or not, this is entirely our fault, because most of us don't vote in primaries; and don't look now, but nearly half of us don't vote at all. Instead, we delegate this duty to those we believe are worthy stewards of the process, saving our attention and vote until it *really* matters: the general election. Well, guess what? By then it's often too late, and the stewards that we entrusted to look after things have already hijacked the election, and we get stuck with, well, you got it.

The solution to this problem is simple. Pay attention early on, engage and vote in the primaries. Start off as we mean to continue, and we have a pretty good chance of getting it right. This is not meant to be a call to action to vote in primaries, because that's just the beginning. The call to action is more profound, but equally essential: we must choose our leaders carefully based on criteria that makes that process more certain. To paraphrase Aristotle, we must focus on what we can control and we can make a difference. We can control our vote, and use a process for evaluating our candidates that gives us the best chance of ending up with a real leader.

Chapter I

Leadership Attributes

L eaders are powerful people, and they can choose to use that power for good or evil, selfishly for personal gain, or generously for the benefit of society. They are powerful because they are force multipliers. They have the innate ability to identify collective insecurity in a population, magnify that insecurity so everyone can see it and identify with it, and then satisfy that insecurity with the promises of a solution that only that leader can provide. Psychologists can discuss what forms insecurity takes, and how it presents in individuals and groups, but all insecurities come down to two levers when it comes to politics and managing a society: fear and greed. Fear is quelled by reassurance and promises of safety and security. Greed is satisfied by continued prosperity and promises that hope, aspirations and dreams will become reality.

In selecting a leader, or choosing to follow someone on any level, as individuals, we all relinquish and delegate to that person a degree of control over our destiny, because we believe they are best equipped to deliver on their promises. We believe they are best positioned to offer solutions to the challenges we face every day, and successfully address our insecurity. We necessarily say to that person, "I trust you to make decisions for me, that are in my best interest, and will give me and us a better future". We are trusting them with our future. That is part of our social contract with our leaders, part of the deal. This is why it is so important that we choose our leaders wisely.

Individuals must have five attributes to be successful leaders. Let's call them Leadership Attributes: *Vision, Voice, Courage, Charisma, and Gravitas*.

Vision

Leaders have a compelling vision for where they want to take their constituents – their people. Critically, that vision must be made their own in order for it to be credible. It cannot be a borrowed suit, ill-fitting and awkward, or it will not resonate with their audience. Borrowed visions do not scale. Vision requires imagination, creativity and innovation that comes from a greater understanding: the ability to see further down the road than others, and the capacity to see around corners.

Having said that, great visions have precedents and are informed by previous thoughts and prior events, as are most great ideas. At this stage in the game its fairly difficult to come up with something entirely new and original. To quote Pablo Picasso, "Good artists borrow, great artists steal." He probably wasn't the first person to say that either. But the point stands, the great visionaries give the precedents a twist, and a new shape that's personal to them, so the result becomes theirs, their vision, which they then share.

People like Steve Jobs have vision. We didn't know what an iPad or an iPhone was, until he presented them to us. Then we couldn't live without them.

Voice

Leaders have a powerful voice to articulate, project, and bring their vision into focus. This means the ability to connect and communicate effectively with audiences of all shapes and sizes, to inspire and motivate. Communication is a two-way street. A great leader's voice resounds, or bounces back from the audience, conveying valuable information to the leader: comprehension, approval and disapproval. A great voice communicates when it recognizes that it is both a sender and a receiver of information, and is able to use the information it receives to refine and improve the message, so the vision becomes absolutely clear, compelling and motivating.

Courage

Leaders possess courage to boldly promote their vision in the face of skepticism, criticism and personal attacks. This is difficult because courage has few companions and is often very lonely. This doesn't mean that the courageous ignore the temperature of the room; they do not. They are often skilled curators, and listen carefully to those around them. They are open to criticism from those they trust, and actively seek the truth. They abhor the echo chambers of ego-stroking subordinates and repeatedly evaluate and reevaluate their position, making sure of their vision. They are prepared to tweak it here and there, be flexible and make the necessary adjustments to stay on course. They listen to their audience, to the feedback, but they are not, however, subservient to polls, pundits or consultants to tell them how, and where, to lead.

Charisma

Leaders have charisma. It is easy to spot but difficult to define. We know it when we see it, and it cannot be faked. Charisma is comprised of passion, confidence, caring and a self-belief, that makes people want to listen to what a leader has to say. Candidates for leadership either have it or they don't. It is a gift and is rare. Like love, it cannot be bought. The trails of campaigns are littered with those who went broke trying to do so.

Gravitas

Unlike charisma, which is exuded and shared with an audience, gravitas is possessed and retained. It cannot be shared; it must reside with its possessor. It rests confidently on the broad shoulders of leadership, is reassuring and forms the basis for power. Gravitas is manifested in wisdom, judgement and certitude, based on experience. Gravitas is even more rare than charisma, and often comes with time on earth, and on the field – in the fray, where the possessor knows that victory and defeat each have their rewards.

The degree to which a leader displays Leadership Attributes will determine the leader's impact and longevity – how good they will be, and how long they will last.

This brings us to the notion of power. I mentioned earlier that leaders are powerful people, and I described why. It is important to understand the difference between power and force, and how important it is for a leader to project power, and not force. Power is persuasive because it is inspirational. It causes people to want to behave in a certain way because they are willingly motivated to do so. Power ultimately obviates the need for force, because it trades on freedom of choice, not the depravation of that freedom. People react badly when they are deprived of options, and forced to do things against their will, and leadership or systems that are based on force, are destined to fail.

Similarly, candidates who merely project competence, rather than power, cannot be leaders, because they do not motivate people to follow them. They are not inspiring enough to cause people to want to behave a certain way. They may be respected, and appreciated in an organization or system, but not as leaders.

Finally, there is always a tension between leadership and representation. Not all representatives can be leaders. We see this all the time when legislators, who have been good representatives, seek to become leaders. They often lack vision and courage. As representatives, they can get away without those Leadership Attributes, but not as leaders. All leaders are, however, representatives, but not of a people, rather of a direction, a way forward. They are guides and earthly manifestations of a calling, a vision for the future that is better than the *status quo*, or the past.

When we evaluate our leadership and those aspiring to be our leaders – whether at a national, state or local level – we should always ask ourselves if they have the Leadership Attributes; do they satisfy our leadership criteria? Do they pass our test for leadership? Do they have what it takes? We should constantly be measuring them against this standard. If they do not stack up, then we should not elect them? Most importantly, we must not compromise in this selection process, because for each compromise we make, we increase the risk that we elect and follow someone who is not a leader at all, and will do nothing for us, or worse, is a flawed leader, who will ultimately take us down the wrong path.

Once we have determined if a candidate has the Leadership Attributes, we need to determine whether they have a set of core values that match our own. Do they share our view of the world and what it should look like? Are they showing us the way to a better world that is consistent with our way of life and how we want to live? Do they have integrity? There have been many leaders throughout history who have these attributes who are bad and lead their people down the wrong path. We can all agree on who they are.

Having identified a leader, we need to understand the leader's vision and determine how good it really is, how well it jibes with our needs and desires.

I have taken the liberty of suggesting what a compelling vision might look like for America today, as what I call the Accessible American Dream.

. . . .

Chapter II

Vision

We need leaders who will get back to basics and focus on what matters to Americans – the money shots. We desperately need to stop wasting time and energy on esoteric ideologies and academic utopian policies, to stop catering to advocates of extreme ideas, systems and processes that don't work, won't work or have already been proven to be a complete disaster elsewhere in the world. We need to keep it simple and focused on what America is all about. This doesn't need to be complicated, longwinded and involved. What it does need is clarity and action. We need leaders who substitute action for talk, and results for motion.

We should all, as Americans, more or less violently agree that everyone in this great country deserves a government that can and will provide the following:

- *Healthcare* that is excellent, accessible to all and affordable;
- *Education* that is first-rate;
- *Jobs* that are secure, enable us to enjoy life, raise a family and care for those we love;
- *Homes* that are safe and secure;
- *Climate and Environment* that is clean and healthy;
- *Foreign Policy* that both protects our national interests and grows our economy; and
- *A Future* that is brighter than our past

We need to get these bullet points right in the first instance, or all the arguments about the details are irrelevant.

Healthcare

Every American deserves access to excellent affordable healthcare; and that means real, complete and effective healthcare, regardless of the medical condition or when and how it developed. Healthcare like many of our services is binary: either you have it, or you don't. Anything short of full coverage, from cradle to grave is unacceptable. Either you are covered, or you are not. No partial coverage, no temporary coverage, no periodic coverage, no loopholes, no get-outs.

This is not to say that healthcare in America should be free. It should not be, but it should be affordable. Like with anything of value, we need to pay for it, one way or another. Whether it is through private health insurance or government sponsored programs, or a combination of the two, doesn't really matter, as long as all Americans have access to the world's best healthcare.

The biggest question around healthcare is how to pay for it. Part of the answer requires that we look at and address two major components: 1) Reduce demand and 2) Reduce costs.

Reduce demand for health care

The good news is, as individuals we have a great deal of control over how much healthcare we actually need. We don't require cooperation from anyone else to help reduce demand; we can all do that ourselves by leading healthier lives. The healthier we are, the less we need expensive visits to doctors and hospitals, and the very costly prescription drugs they prescribe. The answer to a healthier lifestyle is easy to state, but difficult to accomplish. Good things usually are. Better diets, more exercise, and generally taking care of ourselves vastly reduces the need to see healthcare professionals, and subject ourselves to the extraordinary costs that entails.

Reduce costs of healthcare

Healthcare is artificially too expensive, because it is comprised of components that are either directly or indirectly a high-margin, very profitable business. Why is this? Because much of what is provided by many healthcare professionals is unnecessary. Patients are over-tested because tests generate revenue and profits, and they ward off lawsuits. Where one test will do, several are given, in many cases in order to avoid being sued for simply not having performed the tests, whether necessary or not.

Prescription drugs are given because they can treat a medical condition and keep people alive, but they also make money. Prescription drugs are expensive because built into every prescription drug are the costs of potential litigation as well as exorbitant profit margins.

Education

The opportunity to get a first-rate education for all Americans is essential to our continued success as a nation. And that means that each of us deserves the opportunity to develop our talents and skills under the best possible circumstances. Regardless of what form that educational development takes and where it ends, one thing is certain: it must begin as soon as possible after birth, if not before, and must be based on the Judeo-Christian values by which this country was founded and has developed.

Pre-K education is as important to our society as obtaining a graduate degree, if not more so, and we must build that into our culture and our economy. It must be a priority that goes hand-in-hand with childcare, and must be made universally affordable and accessible. Later on, we can all decide whether to pursue a formal education and advanced degrees, vocational training, apprenticeships or other education and training.

Every American should have the option to pursue their education without worrying about the cost and how to pay for it. Quality of education, great teaching and learning environments should be the priority, and cost should be secondary. We should place a premium on great teaching and compensate our educators accordingly. Education, however, should not be free. Nothing worth anything in this world is free. The whole notion of forgiveness of all student debt and free college education is preposterous, not to mention unaffordable to any significant scale, and places an unfair burden on society. We all, as a nation, benefit when our society is well-educated, but that can and must take many forms, and they cannot all be free.

This is not say that there aren't ways to lessen the burden of college tuition, and other training, with low-interest and in some cases no-interest student loans, or forgiveness of student debt, depending on chosen careers. There are many ways to accomplish this, including the use of corporate incentives and sponsorships, philanthropy and federal, state and local government sponsored programs.

The real problem with education in America today is it does not begin early enough, and is not broad enough to satisfy the needs of our society. The education challenge doesn't have to be status- driven, binary and stigmatizing: either you go to college and graduate school, get a degree and make a lot of money, or you don't get a degree and you don't have a chance. College isn't for everyone and that's a good thing. Some people don't need it and some people are better off without it. Education should not be hierarchical, it should be viewed as an opportunity to develop one's talents and skills and to expand one's options in life. But if people know what they want to do, and they can get there quicker and more productively through vocational training, apprenticeships, or entrepreneurship, then they should.

What is important, is that all Americans have the opportunity and access to the education they want to pursue and the freedom to do so.

Jobs

Every American deserves the opportunity to have a job and career that is secure and abundantly productive enough to support a family, help care for loved ones and provide for later life. But, I believe we need to go one step further: we all need to have a stake in the enterprises and institutions in which we work – an ownership interest – if not directly then indirectly.

When we get out of bed in the morning to go to work, we should all feel as though we are participating in the success of our workplace and be valued for it. If it does well because of our contribution, then we should share in the value and wealth that creates. If wealth and income disparity is a big problem in America today, then this approach goes a long way to successfully addressing that disparity. It also provides us with a purpose that goes beyond mere labor, beyond doing the task for the task's sake, or simply because we are being paid to do so. We would then all be equity owners, in some form or another, whether it's stock or stock options in a company, profit sharing in a business or bonuses (in whatever form they may take) wherever we work. The effect on our self-esteem, our productivity and our enterprises would be positive and profound. I don't think we can underestimate the value of a system that offers its workforce, at all levels, the prospect of an unlimited upside. The notion that our earning potential is unbounded, is a powerful incentive and motivator. Consider the difference between an environment where you know you will make (A) a fixed salary and some benefits, *versus* (B) a fixed salary and some benefits *plus a bonus* based on performance of the enterprise and merit. Who wouldn't choose "B"?

Homes

Every American should have the opportunity to own their own home, if they choose. This notion and aspiration has been at the core of the American way of life from the founding of America as a country. In fact, one of the reasons America was founded is so Americans could own their own home. Pride of ownership, is invaluable. It is in America's greater interest that everyone has the opportunity to own a home.

We need only look to the Homestead Act of 1862 to see how important home ownership has been to the development of our nation. The Homestead Act of 1862 provided that anyone who staked out 160 acres of government land allocated for this purpose, or unclaimed land in the public domain, and worked to improve that land for five years, would be entitled to own that land free and clear. This measure encouraged Americans to take the risks to settle further west, endure harsh winters, rugged and often impassable terrain, attacks from wolves, bears and mountain lions, not to mention bullets and arrows, and generally go where few had gone before, with all the challenges and uncertainties that entailed. People were incentivized to leave the sanctity and security of our cities, but they were rewarded for doing so, with an ownership interest in the nation, an equity stake in the enterprise.

Now that our cities have evolved into more complicated, sometimes inconvenient and dangerous environs, the irony is that people who are in a position to do so, often choose to leave the cities for the suburbs and more rural areas. In a way, many of our central cities have become the modern frontier, full of risk and danger for those who live, work or visit there.

This circumstance almost begs the question, why not have a Homestead and Enterprise Act that offers derelict, abandoned or neglected homes and buildings in our central cities, to those who live there, and work to improve and refurbish those structures for five years? With the assistance of local banks, insurance companies, accountants and lawyers, this seems eminently feasible. This would give people who live and work in our central cities an ownership interest in the community, an equity stake in America, and the self-esteem and pride that comes with ownership. Rather than living off welfare payments, or low paying jobs that will never enable them to own a home, they would become owners and masters of their own destiny. Imagine the value this would add to the local and national economies, not to mention the shifts that would occur in society.

If there is a widening gap and disparity in income, wealth and class in this country, this type of initiative would go a long way to closing that gap and making things fair. The beauty of it is, there is not a city or town in America that could not benefit from such a program.

Climate & Environment

Whether you believe in climate change or not, you cannot argue with the fact that we are polluting our air and water, and that is having an adverse effect on our environment. This has a knock-on impact on our health and overall quality of life. It affects the food we eat, as much as the air we breathe and the water we drink. Outcries from environmental activists, especially recent demonstrations from youth leaders, has brought climate and environment issues to the forefront of political debate and to the attention of corporate leadership, who have no choice but to respond with policies and initiatives that address one of the biggest existential threats to mankind today.

The debate has historically, and in my view mistakenly, been centered around the notion of "climate change". This characterization necessarily invites debate and conflict, and distracts focus from the central issue: the environment and whether it is clean and healthy, getting worse or getting better. It is really a binary issue that is not complicated. We want clean air, water and land, not polluted air, water and land. We want to be healthy not unhealthy.

The problem is that much of what pollutes our air, water and land, in an industrial age, is a result of (a) ignorance, (b) "necessity", (c) indifference, (d) indulgence or (e): all of the above. Once we are aware that our lives and the growth of our economies, in an industrial world, entails a high degree of pollution, much of it from consuming hydrocarbons, we have a choice: either we care about that and are willing to do something about it, or we don't and are not. Put simply, utilizing hydrocarbons as a source of energy is bad for our environment and ultimately deadly for our civilization, if the current trend continues. So, clearly, the answer is to reduce our dependence on hydrocarbons, and do so as rapidly as possible without destroying civilization as we know it. We now know that there are viable alternative sources of energy that are renewable and environmentally friendly. The challenge is to incentivize their rapid development, deployment and adoption. For some economies around the world that will be easier than for others. That will create tremendous conflict globally, but strong leadership will be able to manage that.

So, the bad news is, the environment is getting worse and poses an imminent existential threat to our civilization. (We can argue over what imminent means in terms of time frame, so let's just say, sooner than we want.) The good news is, like with most every challenge in this world, we are still at a stage where we have control over the outcome, and we can do something about it if we want to, but we better hurry.

Foreign Policy

Of all the challenges a leader confronts, and must manage, foreign policy is the greatest and most complex, and probably the most essential to get right. This is true for many reasons, but a fundamental one is that foreign policy begins at home, with domestic policy, and the way we govern ourselves, individually and as a nation. The way we manage our society and define ourselves as a nation, determines how we are viewed by others outside America, and as a result, how we are treated. As any astute leader knows, you have to define yourself before others define you, or chances are you won't be happy with their definition, and you won't like the way you are treated.

The answer to how we define ourselves and our *raison d'etre* has not changed in almost 250 years, and can be found in the preamble to the U.S. Constitution:

> *We the People of the United States, in Order to form a more perfect Union, establish Justice, insure domestic Tranquility, provide for the common defence, promote the general Welfare, and secure the Blessings of Liberty to ourselves and our Posterity, do ordain and establish this Constitution for the United States of America.*

If we are strong as a nation, united behind a common and compelling vision consistent with this preamble, and have leadership that nobly exemplifies and demonstrates that, we will be treated with the respect we deserve, around the world.

Specifically, we must have strong borders that define the physical boundaries of our nation and protect our national interests, way of life, and core values. But those borders must be open to those who share our ambitions for what America is all about, and want to contribute to our society in a way that is consistent with our values. For those who do not, or would do us harm, the borders must remain closed and steadfast. In this regard, our country is no different from our home. If we value it, we must demonstrate that, and take the necessary measures to protect it, with all that implies. Nothing is more important, in fact or symbolically, as a message to the world, about who we are and what it means to be an American.

This means we are all about individual and collective freedom, in a free and open society, governed by rules that are fair, which we are willing to protect, whatever it takes, to ensure our future is bright. It is critical that we project this ethos, and mentality around the world if we are to have a successful foreign policy. But projection does not mean imposition. We are not here to be the policemen of the world, to impose our values and way of life on others. That should not be our purpose. However, when our national interests are threatened by others, who do not share our values, conflicts necessarily arise, and visionary leadership is required to resolve those conflicts.

When we think about traditional foreign policy, we think about diplomacy and how we manage our place in the world, and our relationships with other nations. But modern foreign policy challenges extend beyond the traditional notions of foreign policy, and practitioners of modern diplomacy must recognize this.

Some would argue that the idea of a Westphalian nation state as a dominant model in modern civilization, is giving way to alternative systems based on behemoth corporate structures with global footprints. This is dangerous as a future model around which to organize a society. In order for global order, regional balance and equilibrium to prevail, we must have nation states, with defined borders but flexible boundaries at the top. All other entities must be organized in a way that is governed by and subordinate to the nation state. We can argue about what a proper nation state must look like, and how it must be organized in order to successfully deliver on the social contracts with its citizens; we do that all the time, but we must agree on the dominance of the nation state as a system.

Some might argue in favor of corporate globalization, and think it's okay to have dominant corporate structures, but what happens when those entities go awry of the principles of our society, in favor of increased profits motivated by greed? What happens when corporate entities go bad and do bad things? What's to stop them if there is no superseding nation state? Don't get me wrong, I'm all in favor of capitalism, and believe it is the only way forward for growing economies, and modern civilized societies, but I am a compassionate capitalist who recognizes that in order for capitalism to succeed and endure, it needs its checks and balances.

I would go so far as to say we must do everything we can to protect the existence and principles of a nation state or we will head down a slippery slope that does not end well. For instance, what happens when organizations comprised of individuals, who feel disenfranchised, organize around principles of terror and destruction of the nation state and societies that differ from theirs? And what happens when those organizations supersede nation states and cross borders? I think we have seen recent samples of that, enough to know that's exactly what we don't want.

Future

No one can argue with the proposition that we all want a future that is brighter than our past, for ourselves and for our children. The way to accomplish this, and the only way to do it, is to ensure that we choose our leadership well. If we are to thrive as a nation, we must select leaders that have a compelling vision, the bold voice to express that vision, with courage, regardless of criticism and personal attack, and have the charisma and gravitas to garner our trust.

....

Chapter III

Leadership Character

Once we have defined a leader with Leadership Attributes, and we have a clear idea of our leader's vision on the basic topics, outlined above, we can be fairly confident in our choice and move to the next level of analysis. This is where the rubber really meets the road. This is where we ask the tough questions:

- How bold is our leader's vision, and how far does it extend beyond what is expected of a good leader?
- How inspiring is our leader?
- How well does our leader understand the world as a whole, and how to maintain American leadership in the world?

As a nation, we are becoming increasingly polarized, as is the world. And I think that's a good thing. It's good because it allows us to see clearly where we stand as individuals and where we stand as a nation. Polarization is good, as long as it is part of a process, and not the result of a flawed one. I view our current state of polarization as a temporary phase, a layover on the way to a grander vision. It is part of the cut and thrust of hashing out a new future for the country, where novel policies and ideas are tested and exposed for what they really are. It is a byproduct of our leadership testing the boundaries of power and freedom, stretching it to see how far it can go.

I am not worried about it at all, because I sit squarely in the center. When all is said and done, and the dust of political discourse and ideological conflict settles, that's where I think the pendulum will come to rest, the nation coalesces and the solutions are to be found. That's where I think the power resides that is necessary to move the nation towards its best future.

On the left we have the Democrats, controlled by those who call themselves the progressives and rally round socialism, free education, free health care, open borders, globalization, instant elimination of hydrocarbons and taxing the rich on income and assets to pay for it all. The Democrats are currently in a state of schizophrenia and dysfunction because they are struggling to find, let alone agree on, a vision and a voice with the courage, charisma and gravitas to capture the trust of their constituents. They have yet to find a true leader with the Leadership Attributes.

On the right, we have the Republicans, controlled by those who call themselves populists and agree that capitalism is the only way forward, borders are borders and no one gets in until we say so, isolationism works, we can't be expected to halt the world's economy for the sake of the environment, and if we simply leave government out of it all, the capital markets and the people will find a way to solve our social problems. The Republicans are currently in a state of euphoria, some more apprehensive than others, because they have a leader with Leadership Attributes and an economy that allows them to validate, for now, and tolerate, if not indulge an otherwise implausible leader.

By the way, this remarkable achievement deserves some attention, because most people are wide-eyed, baffled and incredulous, as to how this leader came to be. Part of the Democrats' dysfunction is attributable to the outright shock of it all, that has left them paralytic and desperate, trying feverishly to figure out a way to defeat this interloper, this usurper, who has taken hold of the reins and is seemingly driving the four-in-hand carriage harem-scarum, across the manicured lawns of political convention.

Here is how he did it. He mastered leverage.

He made his fortune by using financial leverage. He borrowed more money than he *knew* he would ever have to pay back. Whether he wanted to or not, and whether he should have or not, are questions that never entered the equation. They were irrelevant. He understood the nature of the Wall Street game, and more importantly, he understood human nature, individual insecurities, collective insecurities, where to find them and how to exploit them for his own personal gain. I don't say this in a judgmental or emotional way; quite the contrary. One must be entirely realistic and unemotional to understand the phenomenon; not impressed one way or the other, just indifferent – that's the reality and the way it is – "just business", as they say.

He earned his political spurs by leveraging the political establishment against itself in a type of ideological jujitsu. One by one, he picked off his opponents, by using their insecurities and ambitions against them, embarrassingly magnified in public. He did all of this by leveraging the traditional media against itself, in a third-degree black belt kind of way. First by leveraging their greed for ratings and market share, and then by making them compete against their disintermediation, via the social networks of Twitter, Facebook and Instagram.

The secret is in his name: he *trumped* them all.

What amazes me is that people get so worked up over all this, and find it outrageous. We should not be so impressed. We should acknowledge a game, a set, even a match well played, regardless of whether we believe it was fair or not. Fairness does not come into it. One never wins by saying the other guy cheated, or didn't play fair. One wins by playing a better game, and beating the other fellow on the field.

Part of the difficulty today is that the Republicans have begun to rewrite the rules of the game and are reinventing it to suit their own purposes. And guess what? That's what winners do. That's what leaders do. That's how they stay in power. I am reminded of a private meeting I had with the president of an Asian country, which was going through a rough patch, oil prices on which his economy depended had fallen by 50%, his currency had been devalued by 90%, and his people were not happy. The foreign press was starting to take its pound of flesh and that is what worried him the most. That's where he thought he was vulnerable. I asked what he was going to do about it, and he told me. I responded, "I guess for you it's all about staying in power, or nothing else matters." His response was the widest Cheshire Cat grin I've ever seen. He is still in power today.

The truth is, it's not all just about staying in power. What you do with that power, that position of trust bestowed, and how you use it to shape the world according to a better vision, is what really matters. I believe there is an opening for better leadership than we have today, and I believe that leadership will emerge. I don't think we see that leadership yet, but we do see some of the challenges it will have to face. In any case, we should view the leadership we have now as a temporary catalyst, that inspires us as a society to "up our game" and actively seek a better vision with sustainable long-term solutions to the challenges we face. We need leadership that sees around corners, further down the road, and takes us down paths with maximum optionality for success as a society, that is all encompassing. Worrying about the other fellow's game and lamenting the fact that he is winning does not work. Winners find a way to triumph, and that always entails being more energetic, creative, innovative and imaginative, in short, smarter than the other fellow. That's where the focus needs to be.

Chapter IV

How to Pay for It –
Economic Growth

We will have to figure out how to pay for all the goodness of a vision like the one described above, where, as we continue to grow as a nation, no one is left behind. For all the talk, and to and fro and high-minded thinking, there are really only two solutions to affording anything: 1) Reduce its cost or 2) Find more money. The first is probably not going to happen very easily, and certainly won't happen across the board, and the second can only be achieved by growing the economy (producing and selling more stuff), or raising taxes. I am opposed to recklessly raising taxes, which is what usually happens, so let's focus on producing and selling more stuff, because I think that's the only successful path forward. But first, a quick word about taxes, a third rail of any political ideology.

ROB DAY

I believe raising taxes as a source of revenue for any political body, state, local or national, ought to be a last resort. As a policy, it is an intellectually lazy approach to solving a problem. People who don't want to, or can't think of other solutions, immediately revert to raising taxes as the elixir. And that usually takes the form of rhetoric that advocates "Taxing the Rich". For some, it feels good to say that, and they think it garners popular support, since most people aren't rich. That is fallacious and short-sighted. As a close friend of mine, and acclaimed author once said to me, "If it feels good, don't say it."

Instead, great leaders should be visionary and inspiring, and promote a world where everyone has the opportunity to become successful and wealthy to the extent they desire, without the fear that around the next political bend, or dip in the economy, there sits a lazy politician offering as a quick salvo, taxing away your success and achievements.

When I spoke earlier of the importance of foreign policy, and its complexity, this is where we see it starts to come into play.

I believe it's time to bring back to America the economics we have relinquished to Asia, in particular, China, over the last forty years. We need to bring back to America the manufacturing jobs, both light and heavy industrial, that we exported to China. We need to get back to more product labels that say "Made in America".

This serves two purposes:

34

1) It goes a long way to growing our economy; and

2) It begins to deal with the existential threats China poses.

Getting our economy back from China is a major problem that must be managed. The challenge we face in dealing with China is that no matter how cooperative they may want to be, in terms of fair trade, climate respect, human rights, national borders etc., at the end of the day, their economic power and growth, the success of their country over the long term, will always be subject to an insurmountable constraint: Communism and the ideology of oppression, and implementation of force, that it requires to be sustainable.

Ironically, the more a people are oppressed, the less sustainable the system. It may take a while, but eventually the Chinese people will discover this as they become increasingly aware that the success of China, under their current system, depends upon their continued exploitation and oppression. The only way for a communist nation with a command economy, and a population of 1.4 billion people and growing, to sustain the economic growth needed to satisfy their needs, is for its government to exploit its people to an extent that becomes intolerable. China eventually craters under its own weight, unless it makes drastic changes to its deeply engrained system. This does not bode well for China.

To compare it to a western capitalist system, it is tantamount to imposing a 97% tax on every individual in the country old enough to work – and in China that means children as well. This type of exploitation and oppression, and the complete loss of freedom it represents, is beyond inhuman, and can only end in the implosion of the country itself, as people rebel. In an age where information is efficiently and instantaneously available to all, on their phone, and people can compare their circumstances with those of others, this system cannot endure. Eventually, it becomes clear that the only system that has proven successfully to lead to national prosperity, while maintaining liberty for its citizens, is a form of capitalism. While pure capitalism may have its flaws, it does prove to be an economic model that scales way beyond that of any other.

So, the real problem facing China, in my opinion, is not the relative lack of natural resources, energy, arable land and water, nor the climate pollution and human rights abuses. Those are all major challenges. The real problem is, even once the leadership accepts that capitalism and democracy are the clear path forward to sustained national growth, they won't know how to implement it. They won't know how to manage it and make it work for their society. And it is that fear, and recognition that makes the current leadership intractable, and forces them to cling to a flawed model. Their leaders are victims of their suspicion that they are headed for the economic shoals of disaster, with all that brings as a result, and there doesn't seem to be anything they can do about it, even if they want to.

There is the view that neither America nor China can ultimately dominate the other and any strategy along those lines is destined to lead to military conflict, and ultimate disaster. As a result, we need to figure out how to work together in some sort of global partnership. I disagree, and I am certain the Chinese Communist Party (CCP) does as well. It is clear that Chinese global hegemony is not only a priority for the CCP, but they believe it is their destiny, regardless of what they tell us. No one ever won anything by playing for a draw. In every contest, there must be a winner and in every contest between America and anyone, especially China, I choose America. Anyone who doesn't see that we are in a brutal contest with China is not paying attention.

Take a look at some of the headlines.

China is building strategic islands in the Pacific Ocean to be used as military bases, claiming them as national territory, when they have no right to do so. Why are they doing that?

China is stealing our intellectual property, either directly through espionage, or indirectly through requirements that any business we do in China, be done with a Chinese partner who is then privy to our trade secrets and has access to our know-how and intellectual property. Alternatively, to the extent we use Chinese labor to develop our products in China, we are required to hand over our intellectual property as part of the deal. Do we really need less expensive consumer products at the risk of losing the core value that went into creating those products in the first place – the creativity, know-how and innovative ideas?

China is offering to sell us advanced telecommunications systems like 5G cellular network technology developed by Huawei, which would have access to practically every device and network we use. Why are we so lucky? Does no one see the folly in allowing our largest competitor to operate the networks that are crucial to our economy? Does no one see the possibility of embedded applications that can be triggered later to take control of our networks, or at least strategically disrupt them? Does no one see the Trojan horse?

And what about all the Chinese students that are sent here to study and later get jobs in some of our largest and most important companies? Where is the reciprocity? Where are all the American students studying in Chinese universities and working in Chinese companies?

Shall we also mention viruses that emanate from China, and the way those disasters are managed. It's one thing to oppress one's people internally, which is bad enough in itself, it's quite another to think that suppression of reality and mismanagement of fact can successfully be exported around the world. Why didn't the world immediately know about the Coronavirus. Why didn't the world know the full extent of the problem? We know why.

China is a big problem, and enlightened leadership is required to manage it. Unfortunately, as we can see from our Leadership Attributes test, China's current leadership suffers from a lack of vision, and to some extent courage.

While its leader may have a strong voice, charisma and gravitas, three out of five Leadership Attributes isn't good enough. The archer may be good, but he has yet to discover the true arrow. He is leading his people down the wrong path, and we are seeing blindingly obvious evidence of that. That is what happens when a nation doesn't get it right, and fails to pick its leaders carefully.

The need to bring a large part of our economy back from China is essential, and vital to our future as a nation.

....

Chapter V

International Relations – How and Where We Get the Money

As I look around the world, having done business in most parts of it over the years, it is becoming clear that in order for us to grow our economy, to the extent necessary to address our current challenges, we need to reevaluate our economic, strategic and geopolitical relationships around the world, with a view to both growing and protecting our economy. In short, we need to reevaluate our foreign policy, with a priority placed on our own economic growth.

This requires answers to two fundamental questions:

1) To what extent do we want to engage globally, *versus* withdraw, and

2) If we want to engage, in what way do we want to do that?

I believe the answer to the first question is clear and relatively straightforward. We must be engaged globally, and in this networked world, where connectivity is everything, there is no logic to the alternative. Disengagement, or isolationism, or withdrawal – selective or otherwise, is negligent and foolish. Where nature abhors a vacuum, political powers see an opportunity. We must make certain we do not leave meaningful opportunities to others that could be beneficial to us, or detrimental to us if we ignore them.

The second question is more complicated, but not necessarily difficult to answer. The challenge is knowing where to be engaged (Geography), when (short term *versus* long-term), how (Economically, Diplomatically, Militarily and Politically), and to what extent and why.

I believe we need to build in to any analysis of this nature, a bias in favor of doing what is best for our national economy. Economics should be the principle driver of any decision in this regard. The welfare of all Americans depends on us having a strong and growing economy; from that, all else flows naturally. A strong economy means all American families can have access to affordable healthcare, great educational opportunities, jobs and careers that we want, houses and communities we aspire to, and the time to enjoy our lives in an environment that is clean and healthy.

This is a little bit like soccer. If you maintain possession of the ball: 1) the other guy can never score, and 2) only you can score.

In short, with possession of the ball you can never lose. Since you can never keep possession 100% of the time, the magic is in making sure the times you don't have possession don't matter, and when you do have possession you make it count. That is to say, there will be parts of the world that we can afford, from time to time, for one reason or another, to pay less attention to than others. The ball, in our case, is economic growth. We want to make sure we are always in a position to benefit economically, and nothing can interfere with that. But there will be regions and times where we don't mind if the other guy is there.

Just as we have a test for great leadership, we need a test, or at least a compass, to help us determine the extent of our engagement globally, and the nature of international relationships and strategic alliances.

I believe the answer is: We should want long-term, mutually beneficial partnerships with nations and/ or regions, whose interests are aligned with ours, who share our core values and where the economic return on investment in the relationship, substantially enhances our economy.

In order to determine where those relationships are, we can look at the following Engagement Criteria:

Economics – How important is the area of engagement to growing our economy? If the economic opportunities are large or essential, we must engage. If they are strategically essential to our competitors, we must engage.

Geography – How close to the U.S. physically is the area of engagement? If the nation or region is close to the U.S. – essentially in the Western Hemisphere – we must engage. Correspondingly, we must deter our competitors from engaging in our hemisphere.

Military – How important is the area of engagement in terms of protecting our economic and/or geopolitical interests? Wherever we have substantial economic or geopolitical interests at stake, we must be engaged or be prepared to engage militarily. Wherever our competitors have essential interests we must be at least fully vigilant.

Political – How aligned are our core values in the area of engagement? The U.S. is not, and should not be, the policeman of the world. Apart from protecting our economic interests and way of life, there is very little reason for us to be engaged politically in the affairs of other nations or regions, unless they share our core values and have called upon us to be engaged. Then an evaluation must be made with the fundamental question being: "What's in it for us?"

With our Engagement Criteria in mind, let's discuss several regions around the world and see what results we get. For purposes of this exercise, and to keep things focused and succinct, but recognizing that our interests in the world extend far and wide, and the interdependencies and intricacies are many, I have chosen five regions worth discussing to illustrate the principles articulated above: Middle East, China, Russia, Western Europe and Latin America.

Middle East

Historically, we have been in the Middle East for three basic reasons: 1) There's lots of oil there, and we needed oil to drive our economy's growth; 2) We didn't want the Russians there; and 3) A strong relationship with Israel has been important to us for many reasons.

In today's world, we are now net exporters of oil, so we don't need oil from the Middle East to grow our economy. While Russia has a presence in the Middle East, that relationship is unstable, intermittent and opportunistic, so it is unlikely it can ever become dominant, or even much more than meddling. It does not pose the threat that it may have in the past.

The Middle East is not physically close to the U.S., so it doesn't pose any direct threat to our borders, nor does it offer any proximate opportunities in terms of bilateral trade. As a region, it is, however, one of our largest customer bases in terms of military and defense sales, and our partnerships in the region are important and meaningful to our national security and intelligence gathering programs, so we have an interest in maintaining strong relationships there.

Since we don't have any large economic interests to protect, there is no need or compelling reason for us to have a large military presence or influence in the region. The only marginally compelling reason would be if we are getting paid to be there in order to protect an ally or strategic partner, or to maintain stability in the region, which stability would be in our economic interests. This then becomes a straightforward analysis: How much are we getting paid and what are our opportunity costs? Could we better and more profitably allocate those resources elsewhere?

Finally, politically it is not clear that our Judeo-Christian core values are necessarily aligned with those of the majority of the nations in the Middle East, and it is clear that they are opposite to many nations in the region. The one clear exception of course would be Israel.

So, ultimately, we must ask, "To what extent are individual countries in the Middle East aligning their interests with ours, and to what extent are their interests aligned with those of our adversaries in the region instead?" Because economic growth for the U.S. must be at the top of our foreign policy agenda, we should pay close attention to which countries are actually contributing to our economy through direct investment in the U.S., and where and how they are doing that. Are they enthusiastic and long-term in their thinking? Do they respect us and want to develop relationships throughout the country, especially in rural states, that are not necessarily obvious investment opportunities, or are they merely opportunistic investors who respond only when there is pressure to do so, or when their country is under existential threat from their neighbors?

In short, we must have a clear understanding of each Middle Eastern country's agenda and motives, their partnerships and alliances, the activities they sponsor or condone, and their overall approach to their relationship with the U.S.

China

Economically, China has been our trading partner in a substantial way over the last 40 years or so, and is currently our largest trading partner, with Canada and Mexico following closely behind. China has been a source of cheap labor and low production costs that has allowed us to benefit from relatively inexpensive consumer products, electronics, machinery and other goods.

In terms of growing our economy China is detrimental, predatory and ultimately destructive, but until now has been viewed as essential, if we are to continue to offer the American consumer the low-priced goods to which we have become accustomed. But we must ask, "At what real cost to our economy?" I would argue at a tremendous cost, in terms of lost jobs and the knock-on effect to the communities which have lost those jobs, and perhaps most importantly and least obvious, relinquishment of our autonomy and independence, especially when it comes to production and manufacturing of mission critical technology and products.

We must ask ourselves why we would allow our greatest competitor to manufacture, and control the market for handheld communication devices and other technology that is essential to our everyday life? And if that's not enough to worry us, why would we let them dominate the market for medicines, vaccines, medical devices and other healthcare related, and life-saving products, on which our very existence depends? Since when has it been a good idea to let your biggest and most powerful competitor, control the essential components of your life, your lifeblood? This seems absurd. Yet we continue to think that the low-cost provider is simply that – a low cost provider. Well they aren't. They are the competition, and they are out to win at all costs.

Having said that, because China is so big, and our largest trading partner, we must remain engaged, but rapidly return the jobs we have exported to China, back to America. One cannot, however, underestimate the value of China as a customer of the U.S., and we would like to continue to view China as a valuable trading partner, but on terms that are more symmetrical and symbiotic than they have been to date.

Geographically, China is far away, and that's a good thing, because, as discussed earlier, China is hegemonic in its ambitions and the further away from the U.S., the better. In any case, there are geographically closer opportunities for cheap labor and low production costs with similar or better quality, that are strategically more advantageous to the US, than is China. Mexico and the rest of Latin America come easily to mind.

Militarily, we must remain highly vigilant when it comes to China, and recognize that they view the competition with the U.S. as a zero-sum game, where they do not intend to lose, or be subordinate, to the U.S. Their expansionist strategy is evident in Asia, the Middle East, Africa and Latin America. Their Belt and Road Initiative advertises this. And it does not go unnoticed that it used to be called the One Belt One Road Initiative. Perhaps the "One" part gave away the game too early.

Much of the warfare between China and the U.S. is already taking place in the form of commerce, cyber and strategic alliances around the world. While still relatively embryonic, the threat is obvious to anyone who knows how to look for the right signs.

Politically, our core values are desperately unaligned with those of China and therefore we have no reason to engage politically along the lines that we are kindred spirits, with similar core values, ambitions and desired outcomes. That has already been discussed earlier, but it's worth reiterating that from climate to human rights, territorial expansion to intellectual property theft and espionage, it is difficult to see where our core values and those of China have any congruency whatsoever.

Russia

Economically, Russia is not a powerful nation and offers very little value to the U.S. in terms of growing our economy.

Geographically, while parts of Russia are proximate to Alaska, from a trade route perspective it is far away, and U.S. – Russia trade is relatively insignificant.

Militarily, Russia is a major concern, not because it poses a realistic and imminent existential threat to the U.S., but because it has substantial military capacity, both conventional and cyber. More importantly, Russia has demonstrated its willingness to engage militarily without regard for collateral consequences. One need only look at Georgia, Ukraine (Crimea), and Syria for recent examples. And Russia is willing to be opportunistic and mischievous when it comes to exerting its influence. Look at Syria and Venezuela. Russia is also willing to use its vast and powerful cyber capacity as a modern form of warfare, whether by interfering in elections around the world, or initiating cyber-attacks and cyber-espionage. For all of these reasons, we must engage with Russia on many levels.

Politically, we have very little in common with Russia when it comes to sharing core values and aspirations for our mutual societies, and absolutely nothing to be gained from political engagement with the Russian Federation. In fact, our two political systems are, and always have been, in conflict. This has become increasingly obvious, over the last several years when it has become apparent how involved Russia has been in trying to interfere in our electoral process. With the advent of social media, and the increasingly large role it plays in choosing our leaders, people have become anxious about the influence our competitors have in this process. This is not confined to Russia. We know that Iran, China, North Korea and others with technical capacity are also heavily involved in these efforts. This does not worry me. It should come as no surprise that other nations try to interfere in our elections. That is not a new thing. It has always been that way, and it is their job. It is more apparent now because through social media and other technology, the tools are more accessible and the methods more intrusive. They are doing what competitors are supposed to do – try to disrupt the competition and create an environment that is advantageous to their own interests. But just because people try to do something doesn't mean they are being successful.

We really have two options in dealing with this potential threat:

1) Recognize it for what it is, manage it and not be negatively influenced by it, or

2) Consider it to be an existential threat to our way of life, declare it an act of war and retaliate.

I recommend the first option. In the grand scheme of things, I don't think the American people are so gullible and easily manipulated by a bunch of scheming, programmers in Moscow, Beijing, Tehran or Pyongyang, writing sinister algorithms to try and sway opinion in favor of candidates one way or another. In reality, I think the danger increases when we start to believe that is possible, and react in ways that are irrational and counterproductive.

In any case, I doubt these types of influences can be stopped, in a nation where we value freedom of speech and expression. The antidote, it seems to me, is to be more active and engaged in the process and more discerning; more rigorous in our evaluation of our political process and our systems for choosing and electing our leaders.

Western Europe

Western Europe, essentially the EU, Switzerland, and Great Britain, post Brexit, is relatively easy to evaluate in terms of our criteria. It tends to exemplify our overall objective. It represents, for the most part a well-established set of long-term, mutually beneficial partnerships with nations and/or regions, whose interests are aligned with ours, who share our core values and where the economic return on investment in the relationship substantially enhances our economy. Geographically, it is not proximate to the U.S., but that is about the only drawback. Culturally, the U.S. was founded and built primarily by immigrants from the region, so there is a shared heritage and cultural affinity that tends to bridge the physical geographical boundaries, and a series of "special relationships", both formal (e.g., NATO) and informal that have their foundation in shared and common conflicts over the last century. In short, we have been through a lot together, so there is a fundamental understanding of each other's ambitions, motivations and objectives, and the overall elasticity in the relationships to weather whatever storms may arise, with the understanding that these situations can ultimately be managed to the mutual satisfaction of the participants.

Latin America

Of all the regions in the world, apart from North America (U.S., Canada and Mexico), Latin America represents perhaps the greatest untapped potential for symbiotic partnerships and economic growth for the U.S.

Economically, the region is extremely rich in natural resources, with agriculture, mining and manufacturing being the backbone of its economy. It has the largest proven oil reserves in the world, among the largest gas reserves, bauxite, gold, silver, lithium, coltan, copper, cocoa, coffee, sugar, agriculture, fish, aquaculture and more.

Geographically it is proximate to the U.S., with established trade routes that are simple, relatively short, straightforward and conducive to multiple forms of transportation. We share Judeo-Christian values with every nation in Latin America, and they pose no realistic threat to us militarily.

Politically, Latin America is quasi-democratic, with bouts of socialist ideology and historic flirtations with communism, exported from Cuba and championed by the occasional charismatic, visionary, strongman leader. Those leaders often raise the pirate flag against the U.S., and decry the Yankee imperialist boot, but those initiatives have been generally geared toward crystalizing support domestically and have rarely interfered with the underlying trade and economic international relationships that are essential to supporting their economies.

Having said that, historically the U.S. has ignored Latin America in a way that has left an opening for our competitors. Examples include China, investing in Venezuela, Ecuador, Colombia and Brazil and Russia, investing in Cuba and Venezuela. While Russia's involvement in Latin America has been mischievous and annoying at times, it hasn't been economically definitive in any substantial way, and doesn't pose any real imminent threat. China on the other hand, is a different story. As part of its global growth strategy, it has made substantial, long-term investments in the region, and poses a very real threat to our influence and relationships there, not to mention our economy and our national security. This should be a major foreign policy concern for the U.S. and a primary focus of U.S. leadership across the board.

If mass immigration from Latin America is a major problem for the U.S., it is in large part because living conditions in Latin America are generally extremely poor, dangerous and unhealthy for the vast majority of its citizens. So, they leave for the U.S., where even the most challenging standard of living is way better than the options they have at home.

Seen through the lens of economic opportunity, Latin America is a tremendously undervalued asset, for the most part being mismanaged in a way that gives way to kleptocracy and organized crime, tolerated and in some cases even led by dictators who stay in power by force, exploiting their societies for their own personal financial gain. In some cases, naïve U.S. foreign policy, has unintentionally enabled and fostered these conditions through ill-advised sanctions and economic embargoes. Rather than form bridges and long term, mutually beneficial economic partnerships with our neighbors to the south, we ostracize them. Rather than unify around a common purpose – economic growth for our countries – we fragment and alienate otherwise very valuable partners. Moreover, we leave an opening for our rivals to enter and fill the void with direct investment that enables them to pick and harvest the relatively low hanging economic fruit.

To put a fine point on it, we allow the Chinese to invest in Latin American assets, at a discount of 90-95%, and then watch those assets appreciate by hundreds, if not thousands, of percent. This makes no sense. Why aren't we doing that? This is our hemisphere, these are our neighbors, and those types of economic benefits should accrue to us, not competitors from halfway around the world, whose interests are in conflict with ours. The opportunity for us to vastly and immediately grow our economy and help pay for the Accessible American Dream, is right in front of us, just to the south. By helping our neighbors grow, we participate in that growth, and create a rising regional tide that will dramatically lift all boats.

In short, we need a western hemisphere, united around the common goal of economic growth, where we have compelling geopolitical and national security interests, in making certain that goal is achieved. By uniting our American hemisphere around these common interests, we can define an economic path that leads to tremendous growth now and in the future, both for the U.S. and our neighbors.

Chapter VI

Conclusion

I
f there is one definition of great leadership, it is found in how that leader responds to a crisis. The great leaders, somehow, are able to use their power to get people to make sacrifices for the greater good, especially during the worst of times. They share their vision, where the sacrifices create a tide that lifts all boats. They get people seemingly to put the interests of their society, organization or community above their own interests. In reality, what they are doing is showing people the merit and value of aligning their interests with those of society generally. Artfully, they share the burden of addressing the challenge or solving the problem, with their constituents, and harness the collective energy of their constituents for the greater good. They encourage people to make choices in favor of society. Great leaders inspire and empower people to also be great.

In order to continue to grow and thrive as a nation, we need leaders who are visionary pragmatists; leaders who believe in progress not change for change's sake, but above all, who believe. We need leaders who focus on what matters in our everyday lives, the money shots, not ideology and policy nuance. Not all change is good. Change can be scary if not properly managed. Progress, on the other hand, is generally incremental, foreseeable, and productive. It avoids the pitfalls of unintended consequences brought about by change, especially rapid change.

When we go to the polls, and as we prepare to do so, we cannot do better than to look closely at our candidates and ask ourselves the following: Who are the leaders? Which ones have the five Leadership Attributes – Vision, Voice, Courage, Charisma, Gravitas? What is their vision and how does it square with our own beliefs? Finally, how will they bring their vision to fruition and how will they pay for it?

When we have answered those questions, and only then, we can say to that person at the poll:

"I trust you to make decisions for me, that are in my best interest, and will give me and us a better future".

Then we will have the government we deserve.

Printed in the United States
90584LV00001B/1-90/A